Theory Paper Grade 3   2008   A
Model Answers

1 (10)

(a)

(b) compound
    quadruple

2 *There are many ways of completing this question. The specimen completion below would receive full marks.* (10)

3 (10)

4   minor   perfect   major   (10)
             3rd   octave / 8ve / 8th   7th

                      major   perfect
                      6th   4th

5 (10)

6 (a)   (10)

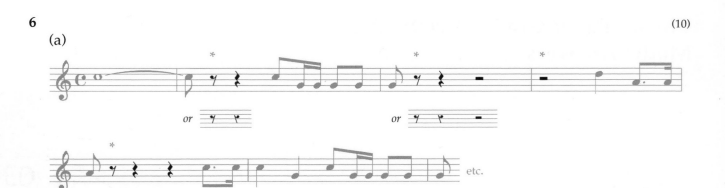

(b) 18

7 (10)

8 (a)   in the style of a march   (10)
              92 crotchets in a minute / 92 quarter-notes in a minute /
                  92 crotchet beats in a minute / 92 quarter-note beats in a minute
              loud
              play the notes smoothly / slur
              pause on the note

(b) (10)

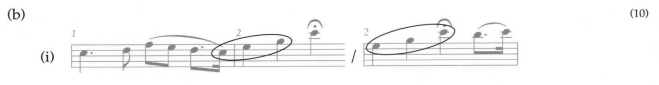

    (ii) C# minor
    (iii) 6th
    (iv) G# / G sharp
    (v) four

(c) (10)

Theory Paper Grade 3   2008   B
Model Answers

1 (10)

2 *There are many ways of completing this question. The specimen completion below would receive full marks.* (10)

3 (10)

4 (10)

5 (10)

6 (10)

7 (10)

8 (a)

    (i)   126 crotchets in a minute / 126 quarter-notes in a minute /
            126 crotchet beats in a minute / 126 quarter-note beats in a minute
       sweet / soft / gentle
       moderately loud / half loud / medium loud
       play the notes detached / staccato

    (ii) four

  (b) (10)

    (i)

    (ii) 3rd
    (iii) A♯ / A sharp
    (iv) false
          false

  (c) (10)

Theory Paper Grade 3   2008   C
Model Answers

1   (10)

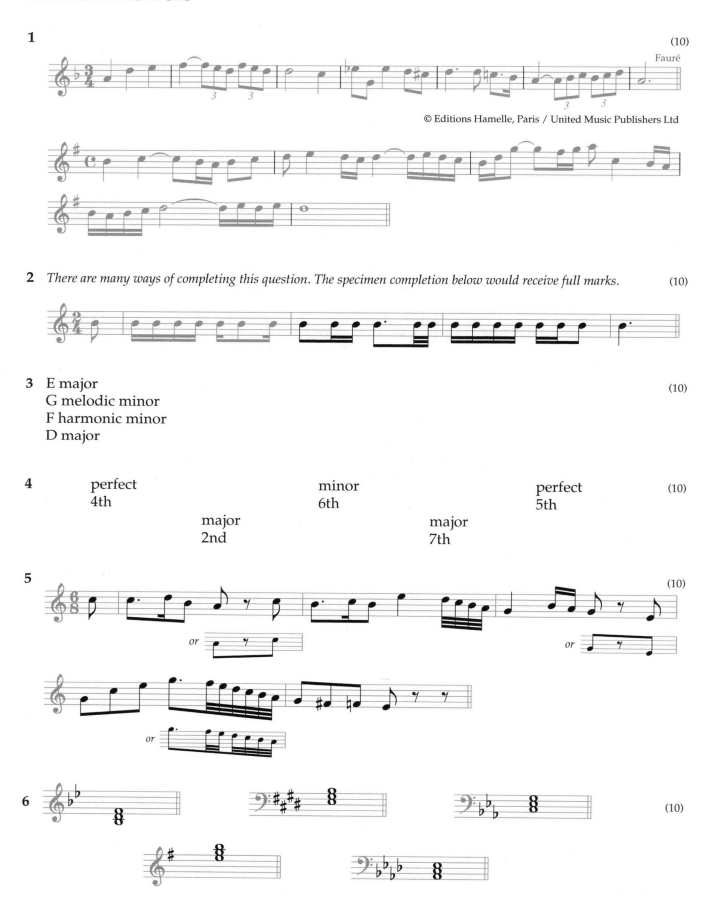

2 *There are many ways of completing this question. The specimen completion below would receive full marks.*   (10)

3   E major   (10)
G melodic minor
F harmonic minor
D major

4   perfect   minor   perfect   (10)
4th   6th   5th

major   major
2nd   7th

5   (10)

6   (10)

(10)

Britten

8 (a) sustained
quiet / soft
always
little / a little / slightly
play the notes smoothly / slur

(10)

(b)

(10)

(i)

(ii) 6th

(iii)

(iv)

(v) Similarity: rhythm / pattern of notes / articulation
Difference: pitch / bar 3 starts a 3rd higher / dynamics

(c)

(10)

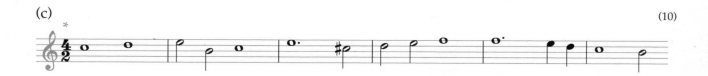

Theory Paper Grade 3   2008   S
Model Answers

1 (10)

2 *There are many ways of completing this question. The specimen completion below would receive full marks.* (10)

3 (10)

4 (10)

5 (10)

6　(10)

or

7　(10)

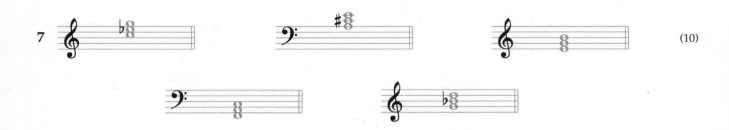

8 (a)　(10)

(i)　slow / at ease / leisurely
quiet / soft
play the notes smoothly / slur
getting quieter / gradually getting quieter

(ii)　simple
triple

(b)　(10)

(i)

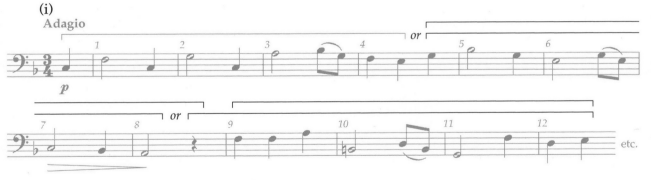

(ii)　5th

(iii)

(iv)　D minor

(v)　8

(c)　(10)

Theory of Music Exams Model Answers are a useful resource for pupils and teachers preparing for ABRSM theory exams. They are available for the 2008 Theory of Music Exams Past Papers, Grades 1 to 8.

Music theory publications from ABRSM Publishing include:

Theory of Music Exams Past Papers
Grades 1 to 8 (separately)

Music Theory in Practice
Grades 1 to 5 (separately)
by Eric Taylor

Grades 6 to 8 (separately)
by Peter Aston & Julian Webb

First Steps in Music Theory
Grades 1 to 5
by Eric Taylor

The AB Guide to Music Theory
Parts I and II
by Eric Taylor

PUBLISHING

ISBN 978-1-86096-983-6

**The Associated Board of
the Royal Schools of Music
(Publishing) Limited**

24 Portland Place
London W1B 1LU
United Kingdom

www.abrsmpublishing.com